Dear
Whoever You Are,

Molly R. Tomlins

ISBN 978-1-64458-429-3 (paperback)
ISBN 978-1-64458-430-9 (digital)

Christian Faith Publishing, Inc.
832 Park Avenue
Meadville, PA 16335
www.christianfaithpublishing.com

Printed in the United States of America

For my mom

Contents

Cloud Nine

Looking back, I'd say downward spiral doesn't even begin to touch where I was spiritually, let alone emotionally and mentally. I laid in my bed that night totally exhausted but unable to sleep— again. Bills, schedules, and sadness consumed my thoughts and kept me from the only thing I *thought* I needed—sleep. Just another night of unanswered stresses and another full day of cleaning tomorrow. I hate cleaning house. But when my part time librarian job wasn't paying the bills for me and my boys, I knew I had to do something more. I picked up a couple of cleaning jobs to help boost my bank account. I was hired to clean two offices and through that, a couple of families hired me to clean their homes. Eventually housecleaning became my full-time job. It was hard on my body and numbing to my mind at times, but it did put food on the table and at least a little savings in the account.

But let me go back to the beginning, back to where I spiraled from.

I was twenty-two years old, and Josh was amazing. He was exactly the man God made for me. His humor and kindness truly were the two very first and most prominent things I fell for in him. And his mischievous blue eyes certainly helped. Josh had a love for God that I did not see in most twenty-five-year-old men. He loved church, loved serving people, and had a heart for kids. When we were dating, he immediately asked me to help him in the children's ministry at his church, and how could I say no? Seeing Josh interact with kids for the pursuit of Christ was amazing. It truly melted my heart to watch him completely dive into sharing the gospel with those in his life. He really met the kids on their level and made the Gospel alive for them. I remember one lesson in particular that he taught. The group of kids we were working with that summer was third and fourth graders, and Josh was teaching about Noah and the ark.

"Now, kids," he said very seriously, "I want you all to close your eyes while I read the part of the story that comes next. But don't open your eyes no matter what because keeping them closed tight will help you really see what Noah was going through. The ark was probably dark and a little smelly from all of the animals."

Josh and I had brought a lot of stuffed animals, and each of the kids were holding one or two to represent the animals on the ark. Every kid was sitting on the floor cross-legged and had their eyes closed tightly, waiting to see how Josh would bring Noah to life for them next.

Josh began reading out of Genesis 6.

And it came to pass after seven days, that the waters of the flood were upon the earth. In the six hundredth year of Noah's life, in the second month, the seventeenth day of the month, the same day were all the fountains of the great deep broken up, and the windows of heaven were opened. And the rain was upon the earth forty days and forty nights.

The kids all kept their eyes closed as Josh continued talking. But I giggled to myself at what he did next. He continued to describe the scene of the rain coming on the earth and what that must have been like for Noah and his family. As he talked, he picked up a filled squirt gun and spritzed the kids a couple of times and then quickly would hide the toy under his chair. Some of the kids gasped and laughed and looked up, but Josh knew who would peek and tucked the water gun away before they saw him.

"Now, no peeking," he said mischievously.

He was *so* good with the kids. They were totally in tune with him and with the Bible whenever he led the group. He was definitely the cool leader, and I loved working by his side. He often challenged me to be more open about sharing my faith with others, but I wasn't a natural communicator like Josh. He was a special gift that God had created.

* * * * *

I myself had become a Christian as a fourteen-year-old at Bible camp, but the depth of my faith was certainly not the same as Josh's. As we continued dating, Josh would constantly challenge me to read and share God's Word with himself or others. I really learned how to pray out of faith because of Josh. I learned how to seek God and glean truth from his Word. It was amazing. I felt totally connected to God and to Josh.

One year after we had been dating, on a crisp summer night, Josh proposed to me. I could not have been more on top of the world. I completely fell in love with wedding planning; and the following fall, we were married in Josh's church which I now called my own. We were both so in love. So bonded. Truly a depth that I had never felt before. Until May 14 two years later, when our first son, Jason, was born. What an amazing feeling to be a mom. Josh and I had adjusting to do as a couple with our new little family member. Josh had a steady, well-paying job as the lead technical support for a hospital in the area. He loved his job, but it was obvious his passion was people, so coming home to his family was an obvious top priority as well as his service in church. It seemed to take no time at all to get into our groove as a family. Three years later, our second son, Carter, was born. We could not have been happier. God seemed to really be blessing our family, and we were thriving!

As much as I loved watching Josh interact with the kids at church, watching him completely submerge into the role of Dad was significantly more heartwarming. He *loved* his family and was the playful, loving, hardworking dad and husband that every woman dreams of for her future. The boys loved being with Daddy; and Carter, in particular, wanted to mimic his every move. I would often catch Carter looking at Josh and then attempting to sit just like him or pretend to talk on the phone with the same gestures, etc.

Soccer was a favorite activity for the three men. Jason showed skill early on, and when Josh pursued stewarding that skill with him, Carter was tagging right along to show Dad that he was good at it too. I absolutely loved watching the three of them work on soccer together, especially because that usually led to an all-out wrestling match by the end. The boys loved family time, and Josh knew just how to lead us in it.

Josh and I weren't without our own struggles, but even in hard times, Josh pointed us to God. His Bible was worn on the binding from frequent reading and meditation on God's Word, and prayer was always the first resort for us.

That is where I was spiraling from.

We'll Never Be the Same

March 29th. I hate March 29 now. It was a gloomy, cold March 29. We had driven separately to church that night because Josh had lockup responsibilities after the service, and often, the boys (Jason now twelve, and Carter nine) had last minute homework to do or a pre-teen appetite calling them home ASAP. I had the boys at my side, and I told Josh I'd see him at home in a bit. He kissed my cheek and said, "Sounds good. I love you."

And off we went. When the boys and I got home, I started preparing our weekly Sunday night ice cream sundae assembly line.

I even dished up the vanilla ice cream, assuming Josh would be home in a matter of minutes. But after half an hour and some melty ice cream, I told the boys to just go ahead and eat, and I would eat with Dad later that night. Half an hour didn't really bother me. Josh would often get talking with one of the other deacons or families at the church and would be delayed in his lockup duties. But when it was fifty minutes later, I got really worried. I called both Josh's cell phone and the church phone with no answer to either. I was trying to decide what to do next when the phone finally rang. It was our pastor. Surely this was just the call to let me know that he and Josh had been in a deep theological discussion, and Josh was on his way home now. But no. There had been an accident? Right outside of the church? My heart and my stomach seemed to switch places, and my head felt numb from the news coming in my ears. Josh had just pulled out of the church parking lot and was going through a green light when a young oncoming driver tried to beat the red light and completely collided into Josh's car. There was nothing they could do by the time the emergency team arrived.

Pastor continued to talk to me, to tell me what I needed to do next. He even prayed with me on the phone, but today I can't tell you a word he said other than "goodbye." There's no way for me to describe the feelings I felt next. I won't even try.

* * * * *

Complete despair, panic, weakness, and emptiness filled me. I sat on the kitchen floor and just held my knees. I don't know how long I was there, but at some point, Jason entered the room wearing his pajamas. He looked at me and seemed very fearful. He asked if I was okay. I didn't answer. I couldn't. He told me that Pastor and Stacy were at the door. What happened the rest of that night was completely a blur. And honestly, the parts I remember I don't care to record here. Pastor and his wife, Stacy, helped me as we tried to explain to the boys what had happened. I don't remember who tucked them in that night after we talked. But I'm sure they were very awake. As was I. My whole world. The love of my life. My perfect family. My top-of-the-world feeling. But mostly, my faith in God seemed instantly gone.

That was four years ago. Jason is now sixteen, and Carter is thirteen. I'm a forty-one-year-old single mother of two boys with a full-time house-and-office cleaning job and, seemingly, very little else. After Josh's funeral, I had tried going back to church. I went Sunday mornings with the boys and Wednesday nights. But the focus of Josh being gone was too much. And looking back now, the feeling of God being present with everyone but me was too much. Eventually passing the intersection where the accident happened was too much too.

I drove the boys to church for youth group but decided I just couldn't go any more. I didn't feel like I could pretend to worship the God who destroyed my faith in one night. Instead I usually tried to pick up at least one or two cleaning jobs on Sundays, so I had an excusable reason not to go. Pastor and Stacy would often call and check on us, but I made every effort to push them away too. Stacy would call and plead with me to come back to church or join ladies' Bible study, but I eventually just started blocking her calls or avoiding her number when it showed up on my phone. Josh's Bible stayed on his nightstand and has gathered dust over the years as has mine. I didn't want to talk to God. I didn't want to hear from God. Now I just had to survive, and I definitely was doing this alone.

But I was miserable.

745 Hickory Lane

A nd that's where you find me at the beginning of this book. Tomorrow I start yet another new housecleaning job. The job was for an older couple who were friends of one of the office managers I cleaned for. Their home was on Hickory Lane which was in quite a wealthy neighborhood; so although my schedule was pretty packed and my body was basically broken at the end of the week, I said yes, hoping that perhaps I would get paid really well.

After another night of not much sleep, I got up at 7:00 a.m., ignored my Bible and prayer time like usual and got the boys on the bus. Carter had been seeming especially distant the past year, but I really didn't have time or energy to talk to him about it. Jason had completely taken on the role as the "man of the house" and helped me a lot with household chores and helping Carter with homework, etc. He was so quiet though and didn't seem to connect with many on a deep level. Jason was sixteen now and soon would be able to drive which would be a *huge* help to me. But Carter—he had been acting out in school, making everything a sarcastic joke. He had embraced his teenager title full force. He fought me on helping around the house and resented me for missing his soccer games when I had to work. He was inconsistent with his desire to go to youth group and even threw it in my face. "Why don't you have to go to church, but we have to?"

I pulled out my handy "I have to work" excuse and continued to make him go. I was concerned about them both but, again, really only had time to think about it on my way to work. After a fifteen-minute drive, I pulled up to 745 Hickory Lane. I got out of my car and looked up, way up. This house was huge. How on earth was I going to clean this in one day even? I grabbed my cleaning bag and walked up the cobblestone walkway to the dark purple door. I rang the doorbell, and an elderly gentleman answered. At first I wondered if he was the butler, but he immediately welcomed me in and said, "Welcome to our home! You must be Samantha."

I meekly replied, "Yes, sir, I'm here to clean for you today."

"Well I am the last person who could point you in the right direction for that so let me introduce you to my wife, Maggie. She's the housekeeping expert. By the way, I'm Jasper."

Jasper was a fairly tall man and very thin. He had blue eyes with a twinkle in them and kind of half-grin when he spoke. He dressed classy. Very old-school. His blue collared shirt was ironed and his khaki pants sat high above his waist. He did, however, have his house slippers on which scuffed across the floor as he led me back to a room in the back of the home. As we walked through the seemingly giant rooms, I was astounded by the beauty of their home. There were minimal trinkets, and the rooms lacked an overabundance of stuff that most elderly people seem to accumulate over the years.

The home definitely did not seem dirty, but I could see why this space would be overwhelming for an elderly couple to maintain. And again, I was hoping for some big tips or extra pay. Jasper led me into a backroom. It looked very much like an office space. There was a *big* dark wooden desk with a hutch on the top. A ceiling-to-floor bookshelf was set in the wall on the one side of the room, and the whole floor was blanketed in thick, cozy carpet. *This will be a pain to vacuum*, I thought to myself.

There was one big paneled window with white wispy curtains and a window seat just below it with a folded throw blanket draping to the left. As I reflect on my first glimpses of this home, I wish I could say that all I saw was the beauty and history this couple had created and kept over the years; but honestly, my state of mind at that time was seeing an extraordinary amount of carpet to vacuum, white thin curtains that are fragile but require frequent cleaning, and *tons* of shelves to dust. I did, however, take special notice of the little lady seated at the big wooden desk.

When the door first creaked open, she didn't look up from the envelope she was sealing. "Perfect timing, my love! I need you to pick the stamp for Kylena's birthday card."

Jasper replied, "Maggie, we have a guest."

The rather adorable lady looked up at me. She was very short and stout and had white thinning hair that was curly. Her glasses made her eyes look slightly too large for her little face, and she had a mint green sweater on (even though I thought it quite warm in the office). "Oh my, I'm sorry, my dear. Who are y… oh dear heavens… is today Tuesday? It is, isn't it? I completely forgot it was Tuesday. Jasper, why didn't you remind me it was Tuesday? You must be Samantha!"

Even in my exhausted state, I found the lady humorous. "Yes, I'm Sam. Nice to meet you Mrs.…."

"Oh, Maggie is fine. You come with quite high recommendations from my great-niece, Grace. This house is our home of fifty-one years, and I hate the thought of leaving it, but I can't keep it how I want to anymore. Your help would be such a blessing to us."

"Well, I will do my best to help you."

"Wonderful!" She clapped her hands together and then turned her attention to Jasper again. "Jasper. Pick a stamp please so I can send this before the girl turns fifty instead of fifteen."

Jasper smiled his smirky smile and walked over to the desk and pulled out the top drawer. Inside was a binder filled with sheets of postage stamps. There were several different kinds: from cartoon characters, to flowers, to planets, to tea cups, to sports balls, to the United States flag. Jasper selected a volleyball stamp and placed it in the corner of the envelope.

"Thank you!" Maggie looked at me and explained, "We have so many great nieces and nephews and cousins and siblings to send cards to that we have come to an agreement that I write the letter, and Jasper picks the stamp. It may seem like my part of the process takes more time, but you should see him maul over which stamp to give each person. Sometimes I think we could just hand deliver them faster."

I didn't want to seem rude, but I could tell that this house was going to take the whole day for me to clean, so I wanted to get started. I ended up asking Maggie to show me what she'd like for me to do if there was any specific instruction. "Yes. Precisely. Good. Let's go, and I'll show you around."

Maggie grabbed her purple cane (this seemed to explain the purple door) and hobbled out of the office to give me the grand tour. We came to the bottom of the long curved staircase leading upstairs. Maggie grasped the railing with one hand and clung to her cane with the other. She made me nervous. She took two steps up out of the twenty-one that I later counted. Then she stopped, and without turning around and looking at me said, "This is as far as I go upstairs anymore."

There was that humor again. She slowly backed down the two steps and then explained to me, "Now Jasper will go upstairs to prepare the guest rooms for when our family comes at Christmas time and visits or if we have missionaries stay with us, but I'm not so sure it's been cleaned in quite some time. The point is, my dear, I would like you to clean the upstairs, but I will not be checking in on it. Just make it presentable for guests please."

She next hobbled into the family room. There were two large recliners and a fire-place and a television. Jasper was sitting in his recliner with head phones on, watching a basketball game. "And here is where you will find Jasper if you ever lose him," Maggie said, pointing at him with her cane.

Without missing a beat, Jasper said, "I can hear you, ya know."

The two of them chuckled to themselves. I remember, in this moment, the distinct sway in my emotions from, "What a wonderful friendship these two people in love have" to "This is exactly what Josh and I would have had and now never will." The opportunity for joy in this moment had just been squelched, and the bitterness crept back in. Maggie must have noticed my change in expression and finished showing me what she wanted me to do to clean the rest of the house. I was very quiet the entire tour. Maggie led me back to the office for what I thought would be our discussion of my pay. She sat in the desk chair and invited me to sit on the window seat. I leaned against one of the walls and barely relaxed my hard exterior.

"How are you feeling?" she asked with her eyes squinting, almost trying to sneak a glimpse of my brain through my eyes.

"I'm feeling fine. I think I can really help you be able to upkeep your beautiful home well," was my stoic reply.

"No no no. How are *you feeling*?"

I didn't understand.

"You are a pretty girl, Sam. Are you married? Do you have a family?"

She went there. I just wanted to say no and leave. But my pay was still not sure, so I had to be extra polite.

"I was married and have two sons. My husband passed away in a car accident four years ago."

"Aah. I'm very sorry to hear that, sweetie. That must have been terribly hard."

"It is," I replied. I hated the implication that four years ago it could be hard, but now I needed to be okay.

"How are your boys doing? Do you know the Lord?"

The two questions combined threw me completely off! I so badly wanted to tell this old lady off for meddling and for being too blunt. But ugh, I *really* needed this money and this job. I took a deep breath and replied, "My boys are adjusting, as am I. And as for the Lord, I used to think I knew him. I'm not so sure now."

I so did not want to continue this conversation. But it was evident, Maggie *loved* conversation. "Well, have you talked to God about it?"

I hadn't thought about it at the time, but no. In four years, I don't think I had once prayed to God about Josh's death. I was just instantly, totally uninterested in any communication with God at the time. Besides, Josh had always been my spiritual leader, and I didn't feel like I could have that connection with God without Josh.

However, at the time, all I said was, "I have not. I really feel like I have a lot of work in front of me. So if you don't mind, I'd like to get started or maybe discuss my pay?"

"Mmm-hmm. I understand. I want you to sit there for five more minutes while I tell you a story."

Oh, good grief. I knew this story would not take five minutes.

Maggie opened a somewhat hidden compartment in the hutch and pulled out a stack of old vintage-looking letters that were tied with a little leather strap. I have to admit that the stack of letters and the secret compartment in the old desk did immediately pique my interest. Maggie plopped the letters in her lap and then looked at me.

"These letters are all from Jasper. He wrote to me while he was fighting in the war, back when we were going together before we were married. Any time I needed to know he was safe or that he loved me, I would read one of these letters and as they came in the mail sometimes with large gaps of space in between, I knew that he was remembering me and that he was really alive and coming home to me soon. I would write to him constantly, telling him all of my thoughts and feelings. Somehow writing these letters kept us alive and together." Maggie looked down. "At one point, there went three months with no letter. No calls back then, no letters, no news."

I instantly remembered how panicked I was after not hearing from Josh for fifty minutes. I couldn't imagine three months of not knowing if he was okay or not.

She got a big smile on her face then and looked right up at me again and said, "So do you know what I did?" She opened the bottom drawer of the desk and pulled out a *huge* stack of letters. "I wrote to him *every* single day! I even wrote the same thing two or three times some days! Even with no response and without knowing if something had happened, I knew I could keep talking to him and, just maybe, he was getting these letters. Writing to Jasper was such an amazing way to connect with him. Turns out, nothing dramatic had happened at all! It was as simple as a new mail system the city had issued that caused a major mix-up with several of our mail deliveries. Poor Jasper probably thought I had lost it! But Sam, writing to him really helped me spell out my fears and confirm my faith in writing that he would be okay."

Maggie then pulled out a third stack of letters. "And these", she said, "Are the letters I wrote to God. Every day I wrote to Jasper,

I wrote to God too. I told him my fears, my doubt, my anger sometimes. Sam, have you ever considered writing a letter to God?"

Though her story was beautiful, I really felt that Maggie had stepped over a line.

"No, I've never done that, Maggie and honestly don't plan to. I just need to work and pay my bills right now."

Maggie sat up a little straighter. I could tell I had also crossed a line. She opened the top drawer of her desk and pulled out a check. She wagged it in the air. "This is the check I was going to give you for cleaning today."

"Was" going to give me—great.

"Now I am still going to give this to you for being here so long, but I want you to do something for it first. I want you to sit there in that window seat and write God a letter. It is *very* obvious that you have some things you need to tell him."

While Maggie was waiving the check around, I could see that it had been written for $100. Oh how badly I needed that money. My tone softened again.

"Maggie, I'd really rather clean your home for that money."

"No no no. This is more important. You can clean the house next week. Do we have a deal?"

"I suppose. Yes, ma'am."

"Perfect. I'll be back in an hour."

An hour? Ugh.

She had gotten me some paper and a pencil and hobbled out of the room, closing the door behind her.

Was she serious? A letter to God? I felt like it was the same as writing a letter to Santa Clause. I sat on the window seat and grabbed a book from the shelf to write on. I felt so ridiculous. This is not what I had signed up for. This is why I liked when the people left while I cleaned. I rolled my eyes, sighed, and put my pencil to the paper:

To... whom it may or may not concern,

Hello. It's me, Sam. I'm really not sure why I'm writing this. Other than an old lady's bribe. I don't really feel like this is anything but a waste of time. I could really use more help with the bills this month so if you get this feel free to help me out. But I'm not counting on it. Hope everything in heaven is going great. Sure can't say the same down here.

Completely not sincerely,
Sam

That took me all of eight minutes to write. I ended up falling asleep on the window seat in the sun for the next forty minutes. When I woke up and looked at the clock, I semirushed to the door. I felt a little disoriented, with it being midafternoon, and I was in a different house. The door creaked open as I walked out of the office and toward the family room. Maggie and Jasper were both there in their recliners. I grabbed my bag of cleaning supplies and announced that I was heading home. Maggie swiveled her chair around and said, "How did it go?"

It was at that moment that I remembered that I left my "letter" on the notepad in the office. I just answered, "I did what you asked me to do." Even though Jasper was watching the TV with his headphones on, he smirked when I gave this answer. Maggie walked over to me and gave me the check for $100. I mustered up a "Thank you." She grabbed my hand and said, "We'll be praying for you this week. See you next Tuesday?"

"Tuesday should be fine." I replied.

I think I might have peeled out when I left.

Some Pictures and A Thousand Words

I n the following days, I really didn't think too much on the rather odd letter-writing request. I had way too many other things to think about. With it being the last few weeks before school was out, Jason and Carter both had big exams to study for which meant I needed to make sure Jason had quiet time to study and also make sure that I had energy to hound Carter to even look at his material. He was so apathetic with everything. School, helping around the house, church, even his friendships. He never seemed interested in having friends over or going to the "stupid youth group activities" as he called them. Nothing seemed important to him except for pointing out my failures or double standards (looking back now, I can totally see some of the things that were frustrating him). He did love to read and was very brilliant for his age.

We were only two weeks from the last day of school; and honestly, I was dreading another summer with no school to keep my boys for so many hours while I worked or came home to try to tackle the glaring needs of our own home. I hated that I felt that way. I wanted to love my time at home. I wanted to know that my boys loved me and loved being home with me. I wanted to be able to relax with my family again or afford a vacation away in the summer. I wanted—well, it didn't seem to matter a whole lot what I wanted.

I'm sure I spent that week the same as many others. I would clean almost every day for several hours either in office buildings or homes. Then it was come home exhausted, shower, see how many frozen dinners we had left and get a tab on if the boys had already eaten or not, half-sleep/half-eat through dinner while the boys were in their rooms, and then worry and stress about my future until the force of the day pushed me into sleep. Sometimes I would think about praying, but it took almost no time at all for my mind to switch to anger or just disappointment in God. I would occasionally look at my or Josh's dust-covered Bibles on the nightstand.

In the first year after he died, I used to feel guilty for not picking it up and reading it when I was worrying; but eventually, all I saw there was another thing I hadn't gotten around to dusting yet, and someday, it would get done. God was pretty not on my radar most of the time and when he was, it was quickly shut down.

Like I said before, I somehow felt that it was important for Jason and Carter to be at church even though I always had a reason to not go. Somehow, I thought they could still profit from God even though he didn't work out for me and my life. I think I needed God to be the answer to Carter's attitude and the guide for Jason as he grew into a man since Josh wasn't there to train him up in the way he should go. I knew Josh would be disappointed in me not pursuing God anymore, but I think I felt that me insisting the boys still go to church helped curb the guilt.

Before I knew it, it was Tuesday again which meant—Maggie and Jasper's house. It wasn't until Tuesday morning on the way to their house that I remembered the awkward letter writing assignment in full. I pulled in the driveway and braced myself for the greeting at the door. Jasper opened the door before I even walked up the porch entirely. It was like he was waiting for me. Jasper invited me in and told me Maggie was at brunch with a friend.

What a relief! Now I was sure I could get things done quickly!

I asked Jasper if I could start anywhere or if I'd be in his way. He said anywhere was fine. I decided to start upstairs and work my way down to the more used areas of the home. I had not had a chance to see the upstairs before since I was locked in my writing cell the last time I was there, so this was my first time exploring the area. There were a few bedrooms and a bathroom that did not take me long to clean. But the extremely long hallway that connected all of these rooms would be quite the task. There must have been a hundred framed photos on the wall in the hallway. They all seemed to be of family. So many frozen memories of birthdays, family reunions, weddings, and school pictures of their (I assumed) grandchildren. Once I finished vacuuming the hallway, I grabbed my glass cleaner and cloth to clean all of the many pictures. The frames were filthy!

I noticed that the wooden frames and glass panels were covered in fingerprints. It took me almost forty minutes to clean all of the frames and make sure each one was aligned on the wall correctly. I have to say, I remember being really proud of my work after that. I picked up my supplies and headed downstairs to take care of the main floor next. By this time, it was about noon. Maggie still didn't seem to be home yet, and I was on a roll now. Jasper came into the front lobby as I was cleaning the floor, and he asked me if I wanted anything to eat. I was really focused and was wanting to finish, but I had to admit that his offer was just what I was craving. I told him that I had brought some food (an apple and two granola bars), but he insisted. I followed him to the kitchen and saw that he had already made two ham-and-cheese sandwiches. I smiled and sat on one of the dining room table chairs across from him as we ate our quick bite. Jasper was so relaxing to be around. As I took way too big of a bite of my sandwich, he asked me, "So how is everything going this week?"

I assumed he meant with cleaning, and once I speed chewed and swallowed, I looked up and said, "Really well. You really do have a beautiful home. I enjoyed looking through your photos on your hallway wall while I cleaned them. It looks like you have a fun, loving family."

"Oh, you didn't need to clean all of those picture frames! That must have taken you forever. Besides, they are just going to get all smudged up again anyway."

Right as I was about to ask why they get so smudgy, the front door opened and in hobbled Maggie, half out of breath like she had been rushing.

"Oh good, you're still here, Samantha. I was *trying* to get home sooner, but you know how Jodie likes to talk!"

I glanced up at Jasper who looked at me a winked at me while he smirked. "Yes, yes, well we were just taking a sandwich break. Sam has spent all morning cleaning upstairs. She likes our hall of prayer."

"Hall of prayer?" I asked.

This time Maggie spoke, "Yep. Every day, Jasper brings down five or six of those photos, and we pray for those people. Most photos are of family, but some are of mission teams from church or other families who God has laid on our hearts."

Jasper chimed in, "And when Maggie writes to the kids on their birthdays, I'll bring down their pictures so she can see them while she writes."

I remember that when the two of them explained their intentional, fervent prayer for people they were *and* were not close to, it really moved me. Those fingerprints on the glass were not something gross to be erased off, but a testament of someone's passionate prayer for them. How encouraging to those people if they ever saw their picture frame covered in fingerprints! I also remember thinking that that practice would have totally been something Josh would have prompted us to do for our boys. But again, God and I were so not on speaking terms.

Surprisingly, Maggie and Jasper let me go right on cleaning after I finished eating. I heard Maggie telling her husband all about her brunch with her friend, and then they both went into the living room and sat in their chairs. It worked out perfectly because I had just finished cleaning the living room before they came in, and so we sort of circled each other as I wrapped up cleaning this big house. My last room was the back-office. All of those shelves—what a task. I took it head-on since I was almost done. That's when I saw it.

On the center shelf, in a metal tray was a wrinkled piece of yellow notebook paper. I opened it up even though I knew what it was.

It was my letter Maggie had made me write last week. Why had she kept it? And put it on this tray? As I refolded the paper of empty words, I literally jumped when the door creaked open. Maggie was standing at the door rather serious.

"Not very heartfelt I'd say." As she nodded toward the note on the tray. "Oh, I hope you don't mind that I read it. After all, you did leave it here."

I remembered what I had written about Maggie. "I'm really not sure why I'm writing this. Other than an old lady's bribe. I don't really feel like this is anything but a waste of time." I was ashamed about what I had said about her. I tried to apologize.

"Ms. Maggie, I'm so sorry I wrote that you were an old lady and that—"

Maggie cut me off. "I certainly *am* an old lady. And honestly, when I read it, I can see how you could see writing that letter as a bribe. But as for a waste of time... it didn't have to be. Sam, I'm going to ask you to write this letter again. And I will tell you that I will promise not to read it or ask you about it if you promise to take this seriously. God loves you, Sam. And from what I can see, you need to talk to him. So since my "bribe" seemed to not be too effective last time, I will not make you do this for your cleaning money. Honestly, you have made our home look wonderful, and I am happy to pay you for that. But I am asking you to take time to do this again before you leave."

My stomach hurt. Half because I was dreading this assignment again, and half out of guilt for what I wrote about Maggie in anger. I just looked down and nodded. Maggie put my check on the writing desk and then closed the door behind her. I picked up the yellow notepad and pen and again sat on the window seat. I felt so defeated. I did *not* want to do this again. But I needed to for Maggie. Then we'd be square.

I took a deep breath and then put my pen to the paper. It must have just sat there for two minutes. I didn't even know how to address it. Then, with Maggie in mind, eventually I came up with:

> Dear -Sir,
>
> I'm writing this today because this very kind woman who has hired me has asked me to. But I have to be honest with you, I don't enjoy spending time with you anymore. I know that you know why. I don't really even know how to pretend to talk to you. I mean, how do you pour out to someone how has abandoned you for years now? My sons are growing and they need Josh... they need their dad.

It was about at this point in the letter I realized I had accidentally actually begun to do the "assignment" Maggie gave me, and I stopped as soon as I caught myself actually writing to God.

> Anyway, I'm not sure that things will ever be good again. But they definitely will never be the same. Hopefully this time I wrote the right way.
>
> Sincerely,
> Sam.

Other than my slip up in the middle, I had completely written my second letter with the intention of leaving it for Maggie to read. I wanted her to be happy and impressed that I did what she had asked and even gave her a compliment in the letter.

I left the yellow pad on the window seat, grabbed my check and supplies, said goodbye to both Jasper and Maggie, and walked to my car. When I got to my car, I realized I left one of my cleaning cloths on the piano, so I hurried back up the porch steps to the house. As I passed the front window that was in the office on my way to the front door, movement caught my eye. Maggie must have scurried in there as soon as I closed the door, and she was grabbing the yellow notepad off the window seat. Apparently she was dying to read what I wrote.

> I just rolled my eyes, got what
> I needed, and went home.

The Breaking Point

The following week was the first week of summer which was great for me in the fact that there were no more ball practices or late nights of homework for the boys; however, Carter and boredom at home meant havoc for me. And I had promised Jason I would teach him how to drive this summer, so he could get his license. That would be immensely helpful for our family, but I was *terrified* to teach either of the boys how to drive. We only had one car which didn't help me feel motivated to offer it up as the practice vehicle, but it had to be done. I would often get angry because teaching the boys how to drive was supposed to be Josh's job. Just another thing God was putting on my plate.

Jason was a very cautious beginner driver. I was thankful for that. We would go out about three times a week to practice. I was usually tired from work, but the adrenaline of fear being the passenger to my sixteen-year-old(?) son's driving often kept me plenty alert during our time together. Every night seemed to go well. Slowly, but well.

The first few weeks of summer for the boys were pretty uneventful. I had continued my normal schedule, and Maggie and Jasper continued to talk to me and distract me from my work while I was at their house each week. Thank goodness, Maggie had not ever said anything about my second letter which I figured must have meant I met her qualifications. Their constant conversation and stories were somewhat frustrating to me at the beginning, but now I actually looked forward to it somewhat. They just seemed so genuine and happy. Two of the most in-love people I had seen in a while. Not just with each other, but their love was so obvious when they talked about their family and when they spoke of God. I tended to just listen (sometimes that's all Maggie would let me do).

One week, Maggie asked about my boys, giving away that she had in fact read my letter those weeks before. I gave them the quick description of our current family but never mentioned Josh or the accident that changed our lives. I spoke to them about Carter and his struggles with authority and peers. I let Jasper and Maggie see a small part of my hurt heart when I spoke about my concern for my boys as they grew into men. Then Jasper told me something that I hope I never forget. He said, "You know, Sam, I have learned that in the verse, 'The Lord giveth and the Lord taketh away,' people often focus on the 'taking away' part. But God *giveth*. I know that in my life, God has given me mentors and leaders when I was falling away from him or needing direction. And I will pray that God gives your boys that guidance too."

That really touched me. I wanted God to work for my sons so, so much.

* * * * *

The day before the boys' summer church camp trip, Jason and I thought we could squeeze in one more practice drive. We backed out of the driveway and headed off. By this time in his training, I was more comfortable talking to him while he drove. We had talked about his future desires some, how he was feeling about summer camp, and more teenage boy stuff like that. It was a Sunday night, and so several of our usual roads were somewhat congested with traffic. Jason came to a complete stop at a four-way stop in the country down the street from our house. I quietly pointed out. "Watch this guy coming on your left."

I still don't know if Jason didn't hear me or just ignored my warning, but he started to go through the intersection expecting the car to stop. About halfway through the intersection, it was obvious the car wasn't slowing down. I shrieked in fear, "*Jason, stop!*"

Jason slammed on the brakes, our seat belts flung us back in our seats after the abrupt stop threw us forward. The car coming from the left laid on the horn and swerved right around the nose of our car sticking out. The driver was a young guy with deafening music playing. The other driver would have been completely at fault, but in my fear and in my tiredness, and in my sin nature, I snapped.

"Jason. What did I *just* say! You could have been killed! We could have... Ugh. This was supposed to be your dad's responsibility!"

I literally bit my tongue to stop myself from saying more, but my eyes welled with tears and my face was hot. I'm sure it was bright red.

"Just go. Drive home." I snipped.

Jason said nothing until he parked the car in the garage.

"I'm sorry mom. I thought he was stopping. I know you don't want to do this. Any of this. And I'm sorry."

He broke my heart. He walked inside and, right before the door closed as I sat in the car, out came Carter. He didn't even acknowledge how Jason moped inside or how I had tears in my eyes. He took one look at me in the car and said, "If you're going to make me go to this camp tomorrow, you'd better finish these loads of laundry so I have something to wear. And am I right in assuming we're just having frozen pizza again tonight?"

I got out of the car and slammed the door closed. I pointed my finger at him and said, "You're going to camp this week because I can't take this anymore!"

Carter shut the garage door on me and went stomping away.

I stayed in the garage a long time. Crying. Breathing. Pacing. Finally, I went inside. I finished washing the multiple loads of laundry I had in the laundry room, and the boys were hiding away in their rooms. The next morning, both boys beat me to the car with their suitcases for camp. I got in the driver's seat which I noticed Jason had left for me and then drove them to church which is where the group was leaving from. As soon as I parked, the boys both unbuckled and got out with their stuff. I was the first one to say anything which was, "Have a good time. I love you."

Jason softly replied, "Love you" but never looked at me and just headed to meet his friends. Carter slammed the door and shuffled over to the bus. I sat in the car and watched the youth pastor lead the group in prayer before they packed up the kids. I waited until the bus pulled out before I left.

I went home so angry. At myself. At God. At Josh, even. If he had been here, none of this would be happening.

I cleaned the office building that night in tears almost the whole time. Then I went home, skipped dinner, and got swallowed in the silence of my empty house.

* * * * *

The next day was Tuesday. I almost called Maggie and Jasper and told them I wasn't coming, but I needed this money and quite frankly didn't know what would help me feel better. So I went. As soon as Jasper opened the door, his smile fell a little. My eyes were so puffy, and my nose was still red from my night before. He reached out and took my supply bucket out of my hand and then told me to come in and sit down on his recliner. I plopped into the cushy chair and waited while he walked back to the office to get Maggie. The two of them whispered very loudly as they made their way back into the living room.

"She looks like she's been crying," Jasper whispered.

"Poor thing," Maggie replied. "Maybe today is the door we've been praying for."

Oh no. What now? Another God project?

The two sat down across from me and asked if I needed anything to eat or drink. When I declined, they prodded more to know what had happened. I gave them a brief synopsis of Sunday night and concluded with, "I know my sons think that I view them as a burden and that I am just a miserable and inconsistent mom. I don't know what to do anymore."

Jasper spoke first, "Sam, can we pray for Jason and Carter with you?"

I sat there for about ten seconds and just stared at him. I went from tired and depressed to irritated.

"Sure. If you think that will somehow resolve this, then by all means, pray away."

I think I saw the hair stand up on Maggie's neck at my snobby remark.

"Listen to me, Sam."

I inferred from her tone that I was in for a scolding.

"Prayer *does* help. Real, genuine, heartfelt prayer to the God who created you and your family does help. God has a life and a plan for your family, Sam. And it seems to me, from what you're saying that God is trying to show you that you aren't able to do this life without him. God has told us in the Bible to 'pray without ceasing.' He says that all we need to do is, 'Ask and ye shall receive, seek and ye shall find, knock and it shall be opened to you' Sam. When was the last time you really were *seeking* God?"

I looked right at her eyes and leaned forward and said, "March 29, four years ago."

She leaned back in her chair. Jasper, in a quieter voice, said, "Don't let Satan convince you that God doesn't care about you, Sam. Or your family. I have been where you are. I was sure God didn't care. But that is wrong. That is a lie that Satan, whom the Bible calls the father of lies, tells us. God wants to hear from you. Can we pray together?"

I really respected them both, but I was not about to pray with them. They could pray if they wanted, but I was going to clean and earn my $100. Jasper seemed so disappointed in me for that answer which bothered me, but I was stubborn.

Maggie stood up and asked me to start in the office today. I followed her back to the office, and she closed the door. She was much more candid even than out in the living room.

"Your family is in crisis. Your sons need God, and they need their mother. But you know what your problem is, Sam? You know that you need God too, and you are choosing to be miserable without him. Now I am going out to pray with my husband for you and for your family. Jasper loves God, Sam. And we both have grown to care about you and your family. But you are the only one who can restore your relationship with God. I know you left your last letter to God for me to read. It was obvious that you aren't interested in talking to God. But I am asking you to take time to really pray or write if you don't want to pray. Write to God. Be real. I will never ask you about this letter. I will not read it if you leave it here. I will not ask you how it went or ever mention it again. But Sam, now is the moment. You have got to talk to God. Tell him everything. Every doubt, every anger, and every fear you have. Be real and ask so that you can find what God is trying to give you."

She handed me the yellow notepad and waddled out of the room. I will admit now that her words and the Scripture she quoted struck me with guilt. Was I choosing this? I knew I couldn't take this prayer or letter seriously while I was supposed to be working. I set the notepad with my things but continued to clean the house like I had planned on. When I walked to the front to head upstairs, I could hear Jasper's voice. I peeked into the living room and saw him and Maggie holding hands and praying. They were naming Jason and Carter. And me. I think that was the first time in four years I responded to God convicting me of my defiance toward him. I went upstairs, finished cleaning, and came down to gather my things and leave. I picked up the yellow notepad and sought out Maggie before I left. She handed me my check and then glanced at the notepad under my arm. She looked at me and smiled a little. "We're praying for you."

I just nodded and walked out the door.

When I got home, my body collapsed on the couch and total exhaustion took over, forcing me to sleep for several hours. It didn't last though. At about 4:00 a.m., I woke up and dragged myself upstairs to bed. My body was still completely exhausted, but my mind was wide awake. I laid there just reviewing the past few days, then years. My eyes went to and fro as I tried to distract myself into more sleep. Finally, they landed once again on Josh's dusty Bible on his nightstand. I stared at it for probably two minutes and felt consumed all over by so many emotions.

I knew what I had to do. I didn't want to, but I just didn't know what else to do. I got up and retrieved the yellow notepad and when I was back in bed, began writing. I wasn't sure where I was going with this next letter, but there was a fire in me that needed to bleed out and tell God just exactly what I thought of him. I was going to tell him everything I thought he needed to hear. With a heart full of hurt, eyes full of stale tears, and a weak and somewhat shaky hand, I wrote the following:

Dear whoever you are,

I am writing this to you so confused and angry. This week has been horrible. And you know what? This year has been horrible. And the last 4 years have been horrible. Where have you been? I totally don't even know if I believe you are still there. Or if you ever were there. I'm so disappointed in the one who I thought was the "giver of good gifts" and the one who gave me Josh in the first place. Then you just take my life away from me? From my sons? No. No, that's not the God I used to worship. That God is long gone from my life. So I don't know who YOU are, or what you're all about, but I know that you have stripped happiness from my family and comfort from my present and future. Did you know my sons are growing up fatherless? Carter hates church and probably hates you. Does that sound worth it? Is that what you were trying to accomplish? Did you know Jason has very little confidence in what he should do next after school? Probably because he has no guide and no man to help him know which way to go. Did you know that I can't even stand the thought of praying to you? Or picking up my Bible? Did your plan for my family work out to glorify you then? I would say not. I'm so tired. I'm so mad at you all the time. I'm so empty without my husband. I committed to marry him forever. I committed and made a covenant to YOU! And you are the one who broke it. Not me. Not Josh. You. I have faith in nobody. In nothing. I am completely unwilling to let people in now. I refuse to acknowledge you in the setting of church where you are made out to be a loving, caring God. Like I said, whoever you are, you aren't the God Josh and I used to follow. I would tell you not to write back, but I know you won't respond. You never respond. I'm so angry at you.

Sam

I slammed the pen down and just tossed the notepad on the floor.

I distinctly remember having two clear feelings at this point. I remember feeling powerful. Like I had finally told Go—whoever it was, what I really thought of him and why he was responsible for losing me as a follower. Then, almost immediately after that, I felt convicted. I felt like I had just spelled out how Satan was winning with my life. There it was on paper. I felt so conflicted between these two feelings of power and brokenness.

And I remember thinking, "Now what?"

Dear Whoever You Are

The next day, I got a message on my home phone machine. I had missed the call while I was out working. The voice that spoke through the machine was Jasper's.

"Hello, Samantha, Maggie and I wanted to invite you and Jason and Carter over for dinner on Sunday night. We know the boys will just be getting home from camp, but we thought we could cook you all dinner and meet the two of them. Let us know. Bu-bye."

I was very unsure about this. I knew Jason would be polite, but Carter was such a wild card and, especially just getting home from camp that he hated, I wasn't sure it was an ideal time to put another demand on him. I would have to read the situation on Saturday night when they got home before I got back to Jasper.

The rest of the week went really slowly. Nothing was out of the ordinary except for one thing. Every night that week while I was home all alone, I wrote more in the yellow notepad. If something came to mind through the day that I was upset about, I would hold on to it and then spew it on the paper. I'm not proud of what all I wrote, but some things included:

> Dear whoever you are,
>
> Today I worked 14 hours cleaning strangers' toilets and carpets and windows. I was so tired and sore when I got home that I can't even contemplate eating dinner. This happens all of the time. Does that matter to you?
>
> —Sam

Dear whoever you are,

Today two men from a local church came to my door. They asked me a few questions including, 'Who is God to you?' I literally had nothing to say. I am less mad at you today. Just so sad. So defeated by this hand you dealt me. But I know you won't respond to my pain. Which just hurts more.

—Sam

Dear whoever you are,

Jason and Carter come home tomorrow afternoon. I so badly want them to come home refreshed and happy, but under the circumstances of their leaving, I'm sure they aren't looking forward to being home again. Remember when my family was loving? And patient with each other? And something to live *for? We don't know what to live for now. We're just so disconnected and we can't learn to go back and be the way we were. We're lost. Do you care about that?*

—Sam

Eventually, Saturday afternoon came. I was supposed to pick the boys up at 3:30 p.m. Pulling into the church made me so uncomfortable. Knots in my stomach grew as I waited for the bus. I hid in my car at the far end of the parking lot so nobody would feel pressured to talk to me. Finally, the bus pulled in. I drew a deep breath as the teens started flooding out of the bus, holding their pillows and looking a bit groggy from travel. While the teens picked through luggage to gather their own things, I tried to get a far-off read on my two sons. Jason seemed himself as he gave his buddies a high five and then headed toward the car. Carter followed behind Jason and looked like he had slept the whole ride home. Then the youth pastor stopped him. Jason glanced at him and then kept walking toward me in our car. I sighed out loud and then thought, *Great, he probably got in trouble.*

I popped the trunk for Jason to load his suitcase in and kept watching Carter and the youth pastor. The youth pastor didn't seem to be yelling at him. After a few more seconds, he stuck his hand out and shook Carter's and patted him on the back. Carter just nodded and half-smiled and then headed toward the car, looking down. Both boys loaded their things in the car and then plopped into their usual seats. Jason in the front and Carter in the back.

"Welcome home," I smiled and said, but feeling totally awkward inside. "How was camp? Did you come home with any war stories?" I was really trying, but I just could not read either of them.

Jason responded, "No war stories for us, but Seth sprained his ankle playing human foosball."

Okay, whew. Jason seemed fine.

Jason went on, "The food was kind of typical camp food. So... we survived. The speaker was really good. We had a service every night, and Carter—"

"Hey," Carter said softly, finally speaking.

I looked back at him in the mirror. He was just looking at Jason. Not with an angry face, just kind of looking at him. I was so confused.

"Did you enjoy yourself, Mr. Man?" I asked him.

He semipolitely replied, "Yeah, it was alright this year but can we talk about it later? I'm really tired."

They both seemed in a fair mood, so I just added one more thing as we drove home.

"Sure we can. I just wanted to run this by you both though. A couple I started cleaning for, Jasper and Maggie, invited us all over for supper tomorrow night. They are a really nice and somewhat quirky people, but I think it could be good for us all to go."

Jason said, "Sure, sounds good."

And to my surprise, Carter said, "Yeah, we can do that."

I really hoped that he would remember that he agreed to that tomorrow night. The rest of the ride home was polite back and forth with Jason answering most of my questions about their cabin and the games and such. Carter really did look sleepy and when we got home, Carter showered and then went to his room and fell asleep for the rest of the day and night.

Jason stayed up and sat with me. He told me that he needed to apologize for his attitude after the close call we had right before camp. He said at camp, the speaker preached a sermon on honoring your parents, and he felt convicted that he hadn't been doing that especially right before they left for camp.

"I'm sorry, Mom. Please forgive me."

I was totally surprised. I never expected an apology from Jason, mainly because he seemed to never do anything worthy of an apology. Besides, I had spent several days feeling bad about what I had said to him and how I'd acted during that ordeal, so if anything, I should be the one feeling bad. I think I was so taken aback that all I came up with in response to his apology was, "Of course I forgive you. And I'm sorry too. I shouldn't have lost it like I did."

Jason just nodded and gave me a hug before going to his room for the night.

Wow. What a turnout camp had ended up being for my kids. Or at least Jason. Still wasn't sure on Carter. I picked up my yellow notepad that night and wrote:

Dear whoever you are,

Finally I caught a break. My boys came home from camp relaxed and seemingly in a much better headspace than when they left. It's amazing what a week-long vacation will do. IF you had anything to do with Jason's apology tonight, I appreciate it, but again, I'm sure just having some time away was what he needed. Hopefully this lasts so our family can have some collective peace for a while. Please just let us have this victory for a while. Just let us be able to endure each other and have a peaceful home even if it isn't like it used to be. Or you could just leave us alone and maybe we can just carry on through just fine. Whatever it takes.

—Sam

Lasagna Night

The next day was Sunday and after I dropped the boys off at church, I went to work until they needed to be picked up. After we all got home that afternoon, I reminded them that Jasper and Maggie were having us over that night. They both seemed to remember and was fine with it.

For some reason, I was excited for this. I don't know why, but I just felt so much love from Jasper and Maggie and really felt that the boys would soak up that type of connection that we seemed to have lost. Jasper opened the door when we arrived and greeted us with a typical sparkly-eyed grin and a,

"Hello Samantha! These young men must be the young men we've been waiting to meet!"

I smiled and introduced Jason and Carter to Jasper. Jasper poked out his hand and shook hands with them both. Jasper was a character but the height of a gentleman. "Either of you boys need a homemade cookie? Snickerdoodle?"

I remember noticing that Carter chuckled at that offer. And not in a "I'm too cool for that" kind of way, I think he just thought Jasper was amusing. Both boys took him up on the offer, and Jasper clapped his hands and scooted off to the kitchen with the boys close behind. Maggie met me in the front lobby and grabbed my hands. "We're so glad you all are here," she said with a big smile. "Jasper's already on cookie duty, I take it? I told him we should really wait until after we've eaten, but he does love to spoil anyone who walks through the front door as I'm sure you've noticed."

Maggie snagged my hand once again and walked with me into the kitchen where we saw the three men standing around the kitchen island, talking with evidence of cookie consumption everywhere. Jasper introduced the boys to Maggie, and then Maggie stated the first surprise of the night. "Well I know you all came over for dinner tonight, but unfortunately, we have none."

I shot a glance at Carter first who I knew would be annoyed by Maggie's opening comedy before dinner. But he seemed just as confused like Jason and me. Jasper was smiling and gave me a mischievous wink, so I knew something was afoot. I leaned back and glanced at the dining room table; and sure enough, there was no food. Not even empty place settings. Then Maggie continued, "Tonight we're cookin' what we're eatin. I wasn't exactly sure what you all would like to eat, so we just thought we'd make it a team effort and cook the ultimate meal together. Jasper, tell the gang what the options are."

Jasper smirked and gave his list. It was fairly obvious this had been a rehearsed routine, but Jason and Carter seemed somewhat amused by it even though I hadn't heard either of them say more than a "hello, nice to meet you" since we walked in. Jasper gave use the options of homemade pizza (which I could see both of the boys' shudder at from their frozen pizza intake lately), oven-baked subs, toss salads (another shudder from the boys), lasagna, or shredded chicken sandwiches.

The boys voted for lasagna, and I agreed. I knew it'd be interesting seeing the boys cook. It'd be even more interesting seeing Jasper and Maggie cook with the boys and me, but off we went. Naturally, Maggie had all of the ingredients for homemade lasagna; and soon, we were in an assembly line of boiling pasta noodles and then layering our masterpiece meal. I hadn't realized it, but my sons at the time didn't even know how to boil the water! I loved watching Jasper and Maggie interact with Jason and Carter as they explained the ins and outs of their "famous" lasagna. They scurried around the kitchen and showed the boys how to cook the meat on the stove top, boil the pasta, etc. I was surprised that it only took about ten minutes for Jason and Carter to open up to them and start participating in the conversation.

Maggie showed Jason how to grate fresh parmesan without "shredding his fingers." That thought made me squint and twinge with the thought of pain. I began buttering bread slices for garlic bread while Jasper and Carter continued the layering. Jasper was telling all kinds of stories about when he was overseas and all they had to eat was crackers and water. Maggie told us that the sauce they were now pouring over the top of the mile-high lasagna was a top secret recipe.

"Is there a secret ingredient?" Carter asked.

"Oh yes. I'm sure there is," Maggie responded.

"What is it?" Jason was already grinning, waiting for the punchline which Jasper delivered.

"She'd have to write to Prego to find out what it is."

Everyone had a laugh, including me. This was the most family time I had had in a very long time; and the weirdest part was, my sons seemed to be enjoying themselves! I was thrilled that these two people I worked for would take such time with my family. I was touched.

Of course the lasagna took forty minutes to bake, so Jasper invited us all into the living room to sit down after our tireless efforts. But not before Maggie showed the boys how to set the table "the right way" with forks on the left and knives and spoons on the right, etc.

It was obvious this part of the activity wasn't as fun as the cooking part for them, but they were good sports about it. After the table was set, we went to sit and talk until it was time to eat. Maggie and Jasper sat in their recliners, and we three sat on the couch.

"So your mom tells us you just went to church camp. How was it?" Maggie inquired.

Jason spoke first, telling them all about his cabin mates and the games and the good food they had. He told them pretty much everything he had told me about camp.

"And did you have fun Carter?" Jasper asked.

This would be the start of the negativity for the night I had a feeling. Carter rarely had anything good to say about camp—or anything. But he just quietly answered, "Yeah, I did. It was a lot different from the last couple of years."

That was another surprise of the night.

After a little more prodding from Jasper, Carter shared that he really enjoyed his camp cabin counselor and the special speaker of the week. He went on to say, "There was a really good sermon on God's love and how we are supposed to love others with the love God has shown us. He preached a lot from John, and I am reading John now."

It was a good thing Jason was in between Carter and me on the couch because I started to slightly tear up. I wanted to just lean over awkwardly and say, "Why didn't you tell me that?" But I just kept listening.

Jasper asked him if he had any scripture on love memorized, and Carter actually said, "I am working on John 3:34–35. 'A new commandment I give unto you, that ye love one another; as I have loved you, that ye also love one another. By this… '"

Carter struggled to remember the rest, but Jasper jumped in and finished, "By this shall all men know that ye are my disciples, if ye have love one to another."

"Yeah," Carter meekly replied.

I was totally floored. That was kind of the end of the spiritual discussion. Maggie went on to ask the boys if our house was as clean as theirs was because, "Your mom does such a marvelous job when she comes and cleans our house."

Carter literally snickered out loud, and Jason tried to politely cover for me, but I finally chimed in and just admitted defeat when it came to our house. I laughed and said I lived a double life when it came to cleaning. Jason chimed in, "Yeah, if our house was Mom's resume, she may not get hired."

The room chuckled. Usually that comment would have stung a little bit, but we all seemed so relaxed that I laughed out loud at his witty comment (besides, he was completely right).

It wasn't long after that that the timer went off for the lasagna. Jason and Maggie went to check it and top it with cheese, leaving a clear line of sight from me to Carter. I was no longer fighting back tears, but I still had to look at him and smile.

He looked at me and quickly then looked away. Apparently I made him uncomfortable. The smile was too much.

Finally we got the call to come to the table to eat! I will admit, I was starving! After we were all seated, Jasper said he was going to pray over the meal.

"Dear, Heavenly Father, we just thank you for this food that you allowed us to prepare and for the company who are here to help us eat it. We ask that you would guide us and protect us in the days to come. God, we love you. Amen."

The moment Jasper said amen, Maggie stood up and said, "Now before we dig in, I want a picture!"

If there was one more delay from bringing this food to my mouth, I was going to just fall over!

Maggie told me to stand between Jason and Carter and yes, the lasagna. She took a quick snapshot with her disposable camera. She held up her camera and proudly said, "Dollar ninety-nine at the drug store."

Finally we got the okay to cut into our work of art, and I have to admit, it was amazing! Maybe it was just the starving tactic, but it tasted so good to have homemade food.

The conversation was less at dinner because we all were busy filling our hungry bellies. But among all of the clinking silverware and sipping of water, I just glanced around the table and felt so thankful. And in my head I just thanked—well whoever it was for tonight and for Maggie and Jasper.

I think that night was one of the first nights in a long time that all three of us were having a good time at the same time. I knew that Maggie and Jasper were the reason for that. Their instant love and care for my family—*hmm, my family*— Their instant love and care for us pulled us in like a magnet.

We were hooked.

Where are You Casting?

I n the following weeks, I did not do much
writing to God. As I think about it now,
I think it was because that night at Maggie
and Jasper's house, I felt a softening toward
whoever it was, and my stubbornness wanted
to strengthen my bitterness a little bit longer.
Jason was noticeably helping more now that it
was summer, and his driving was really coming along well. I still was extremely stressed
getting in the car to teach him, but he really
did have a knack.

The biggest changes were in Carter. We
never did talk again about what he learned
from camp in the weeks before regarding
God's love. I knew bringing it up to him

would just shut him down, and frankly, I just wanted to ration as much of his better attitude as possible. He wasn't an angel by any means, but he just seemed a bit more grounded. He wasn't fighting me on going to church unless it was because of the early hour on Sundays. And he started talking a lot more about Pastor Dave and his son Tyler from church. Pastor Dave was the youth pastor and was the man I saw talking with Carter when I picked him up from camp. They seemed to be forming a bond which was great in my eyes. Carter needed some friends. And if it got him to not fight me in the church area, I was even more grateful.

The three of us continued to visit with Maggie and Jasper every once in a while. Jasper had the boys over to help him do yardwork while I would clean and chat with Maggie. She was becoming a dear friend. I grew to enjoy her stories of life and love with Jasper. I really only felt tuned out when she would tell me how God had blessed them. Then I felt the comparison come on, and I'd shut down. As long as I could dodge the God conversation with her, I really enjoyed our talks. One day, I was cleaning upstairs in their home when I noticed something different about the hall of prayer pictures. There was one photo added at the end of the hall. As I walked closer, my eyes began to well up with tears. The photo frame, covered in fingerprints from frequent prayer, held the photo of Jason, Carter, and me. It was the photo Maggie snapped the night we made lasagna with them. Knowing that Maggie wouldn't be coming upstairs, I allowed myself to cry. It felt so amazing to be loved by these two people. And I now had the evidence of what I had probably known all along which was that Maggie and Jasper had been intentionally presenting me and the boys to God. Most likely begging him to rescue us. I remember thinking that they were probably doing what I used to do. They were probably asking God to help Carter's attitude, provide me with money for our lives, and keep the car running so I could keep working. I just hoped God heard them more than he seemed to hear me.

After almost two months of summer were gone, I got the notice that the main office building I cleaned for was closing down and would no longer be needing my services. They didn't seem to care that I needed them to need my services. This building alone was about a quarter of my income and had no other jobs lined up to replace it. The stress of being the only financial provider flooded me again. Jason had gotten a job at the local sub shop, but I knew his money had to be dedicated for his college tuition. College tuition. That is something else that would so much better covered if Josh were here. I was thrilled that Jason wanted to go to college, but I had nothing. No ounce left in me to help him with paying for higher education.

And now with this job giving me up, I was so depressed.

Christmas would be even worse this year, birthdays would be a cake at best, and we would have to even talk about Carter giving up soccer camp that was the week before school started. When I presented that possibility to Carter, he was furious. This was the first major outburst I had seen since the return from camp. He yelled at me and told me that soccer camp was the *one* thing he was counting on, and he had to participate to get ready for tryouts at school. I tried to explain (more harshly than I needed to) that I had no way to pay for it right now. He stormed off and just went up to his room. I was devastated. Why was this happening? And why did *this* seem to be the one millionth *this* that had happened to us? How on earth was I supposed to do this for the rest of my life?

That week at Maggie and Jasper's, I was quiet. Partially from stress, partially from tiredness, and partially because I think I wanted Maggie to ask me what was wrong so she could tell me that she would help us or tell me what to do. She did both. But not in the way I was expecting.

After I had finished cleaning, we went to her office room. She was at her desk, and I claimed the window seat that I now viewed as my spot during our chats. It was an especially warm summer day, so the sun sunk into my back and glistened off of Maggie's rhinestone pin she wore on her shirt. Maggie had sensed that something was wrong, and so I started to explain the job situation and Carter's anger about soccer camp. I told her how depressed I felt again and how I just knew it'd never get better. I looked up at her in search of tearful, compassionate eyes but found myself somewhat startled because her eyes were neither tearful nor compassionate. She was practically glaring at me and seemed a tad putout. I wasn't sure what to do with this reaction.

"So… that's it. I just don't know what to do."
I prodded.

But Maggie didn't budge. She just nodded her head and glanced at the floor. Finally
she spoke, "Sam, have you written to God
lately?"

*Are you kidding me? This again? This is
your response to my problems?*

"No, Maggie. That didn't seem to help
much." I sighed the words out.

Maggie was not sympathetic at all it
seemed like.

"Sam, I have been thinking about you a
lot. I am so grateful that God has led us to
each other."

(She didn't act like it at this moment.)

"*But,*" she went on, "You have got to stop
coming to me with these trials. I am not God.
And I am not your intercessor to God. You need
to talk to God. Pray, write, sing, something. You
need to truly seek God. Tell him. Tell him what
is hard for you. And tell him what is good. First

Peter 5:7 says, 'Casting all your care on him; for he careth for you.' All means all, Sam. From now on, I really want you to talk to God before you talk to me about any of these things. I love you, sweetheart, but I am afraid I am allowing you to avoid God by being your go-to during these trials. I want to talk with you and help you find solutions to these hardships. But I cannot be in line before God in your emergency contacts. God loves you so much, Sam. He is desperately wanting to hear you and help you. Just go to him. Please take this the right way."

I did not take it the right way. I was hurt and offended and felt judged that I wasn't being upset the right way. I just stood up, blood pressure high, and said, "Thanks for listening. I'll be here next week to clean."

I swiped my check off the desk and walked out with my things.

I am pretty sure I shut the door a
bit harder than I needed to.

Finally an Answer

That night at home, it was just me. Carter had gone out with Pastor Dave and his son Tyler and Jason was working. I walked upstairs and after a shower, I got ready for bed. It was only 8:30 p.m., but I wanted to retire the day. I flung the sheets back and saw that stupid yellow notepad on the floor next to my slippers.

Fine Maggie. I'll do it your way. I will write to—whoever it is.

I knew as I started to write that this one would be a doozy. Maggie said God wanted to hear from me, so he was going to hear from me. I started the letter as usual,

Dear whoever you are—

Then I stopped. I took a deep breath and remembered more of Maggie's words. She had quoted First Peter 5:7 and told me to cast all my cares on God because He cared for me. My wheels began to turn. I would prove that God didn't care. I would write to God. I would cast ALL my cares on HIM. And then, when He didn't answer again, I would show Maggie why I didn't need to talk to God when He never came through for me. He didn't want to hear from me.

I turned to the next page and started over.

Dear God,

Today I am writing to you to prove that you aren't listening. I don't even mind writing this out to you because I know you won't read this or answer it. I was challenged to write to you and tell you "all my cares." Well, I hope you're ready. Here is the list.

DEAR WHOEVER YOU ARE,

1. I lost one of my biggest cleaning jobs and will never be able to make a living for me and my kids without it.

2. Carter hates me and is devastated that he won't be able to go to soccer camp.

3. Jason is saving for college and will probably never be able to follow that dream because I can't help him.

4. My only friends are in their eighty's and today I was told that I can't even talk to them about my life before I talk to you.

5. My house is a wreck. It is totally trashed and I'll never have time to be on top of it.

6. I miss my husband.

I stopped my pen here for a long time. A very long time. This one was hard. But I kept going.

I miss having his hand to hold. I miss seeing him raise his sons. He was the only one who could tell me that it would be alright and I believed him. I miss falling asleep feeling secure with him instead of afraid without him. I miss having the time to make his home a place of comfort instead of contention. I miss Josh driving us to church every week and hearing him sing songs on the way there even if I was a bit cranky in the mornings. I miss family nights with him. I miss being loved.

7. *I HATE cleaning. And it's all I have and NOW I can't even find enough cleaning to pay the bills.*

8. I miss believing in you. I miss feeling like you were real. Like you cared for me. For my family.

9. I don't feel like we're a complete family. I hate saying we are a family of 3. We were supposed to have Josh and be a family of 4.

10. I am so mentally exhausted all the time. I just want to have peace!

11. I remember the night Josh died, Pastor talked to me about Job and how God was going to use this trial in my life just like he used Job's. I don't WANT to relate to Job. I don't want to know what he felt or how he grew. I don't want to need you.

12. I am so tired of being disappointed by you. I'm so tired of not hearing from you. I can't count on you.

Those are the main things for now. I'm sure I will think of more, but right now I have to lie down and try to figure out in my head how we are going to make it—Again.

I used to feel like I knew you. Like we had a relationship. But how do I have a relationship with someone who doesn't respond to my deepest pain? How do I follow that person?

Sincerely,
Sam

The next day was supposed to be my big office building day, but with that no longer an option, I just stayed home and looked through the newspapers for job postings. I got a call at about 9:00 a.m. It was Jasper. He wanted me to come over if I wasn't busy. Well I was anything but busy. I felt a little uncomfortable going over there after my last conversation with Maggie, but at the same time, I felt prepared to show her my letter and prove to her that God wasn't who I needed to talk to.

When I got there, Jasper invited me in and we sat in the living room. They both took their recliners, and I sat on the couch with the letter in my pocket. Jasper leaned forward a little and said, "Maggie talked to me about what she told you yesterday. Sam, we pray for you and Jason and Carter every day."

Every day? My spine wasn't quite so stiff after he told me that.

"We just wanted to encourage you by telling you that God wants to hear from you too. We will keep praying for you all every day, but God needs to hear from all of his children. Remember the verse we talked about? 'Ask and it shall be given, seek and ye shall find, knock and it shall be opened until you.'"

Jasper had challenged me with that verse one of my first weeks there. Maggie added, "We wanted to help you ask, seek, and knock, Sam. Then see what God will do."

This was my moment. I felt so moved by their compassion during this conversation, but I needed them to see that God didn't treat me like he treated them. I pulled out my letter and saw a glimmer of satisfaction in Maggie's eye when she realized what it was.

"Maggie, I wrote this to show you. These are my cares. Last night, I cast them on God. But I woke up this morning, and you know what? They are all the same. They have been the same for the most part, for years. God doesn't hear my knock, he doesn't show me what I seek, and he doesn't answer what I ask."

Maggie said one thing that froze me, "Where have you been seeking?"

I had nothing to say. I felt like the junior high student who was called on in class while they were day dreaming. All I could come up with was, "Well I hunted through the newspaper for job postings, and nothing is out there."

I knew that was a horrible answer. Jasper spoke next, "Sam, have you looked in the letter God wrote you?"

He picked up his Bible and held it out to me and then said, "I want you to take this right now and then read to us one of the cares on your list to God."

I opened my letter. I chose number 7 because I thought for sure there would be no answer in the Bible to, "I *hate* cleaning. And it's all I have, and *now* I can't even find enough cleaning to pay the bills."

Jasper asked me to look up Philippians 4:19 and read it out loud. I read. "But my God shall supply all your need according to his riches in glory by Christ Jesus."

My eyes didn't look up. I hadn't read the Bible at all, let alone out loud, for years. Jasper softly said, "Sam, God promises in that verse that he is going to supply you with *all* you need. I can't tell you how he's going to do it, but I *know* he is going to meet your needs because he promised it. Read another one."

My eyes stayed down and, with a slightly quivering hand and voice, I read number 10. "I am so mentally exhausted all the time. I just want to have peace!"

Jasper asked me to read Psalm 23:1–4.

> The Lord is my shepherd; I shall not want. He maketh me to lie down in green pastures: he leadeth me beside the still waters. He restoreth my soul: he leadeth me in the paths of righteousness for his name's sake. Yea, though I walk through the valley of the shadow of death, I will

fear no evil: for thou art
with me; thy rod and thy
staff they comfort me.

Then Philippians 4:7, "And the peace of God, which passeth all understanding, shall keep your hearts and minds through Christ Jesus."

A tear sneaked down my cheek as Maggie lovingly said, "God answered your letter before you even wrote yours, Sam."

Jasper and Maggie talked with me for a long time that day. They walked through more of the cares on my list with me but encouraged me to go home and read God's letter to me for myself also. Before I left, they both shuffled over to the couch and sat on either side of me. Maggie held my hand, and Jasper put his hand on my shoulder while he prayed out loud. I honestly can't remember most of his prayer. I was feeling so overwhelmed by emotions and by the life I was seeming to regain spiritually.

It was amazing and terrifying. I didn't want to trust God again, but somehow, I was trying to. It was such a conflict, but I needed to try now. I remember thinking, as Jasper prayed, that Josh would have been right there with me encouraging me to go home and dive into God. And that's just what I did.

That night, I made sure the boys were all set with dinner. We had an abundance of lasagna the past few weeks since Jason and Carter felt like they had mastered the signature recipe. I told them I loved them and I had something very important to do, and I went up to my room. I sat on my bed and looked to my right. There sat my dusty Bible. No abundance of fingerprints like the pictures prayed over in Jasper and Maggie's house. I took out my letter and, with a deep breath, picked up my Bible.

I used my hand to wipe off the dust from the front cover. I spent four hours that night just reading the words that God had written centuries ago; but somehow, they seemed so personal, and many of the passages I read directly answered my "cares" in my letter. I wrote down a lot of what I read. Especially those passages that answered my deep hurts or worries I listed in my letter. I felt like God was answering my "ask," and I was finding what I had been claiming I was "seeking." God was real again.

That night I prayed. For the first time since Josh's death, I prayed. It wasn't long, and it wasn't hurt-free, but I prayed.

> That night, I fell asleep with the same list of cares I had the night before but with an entire notepad full of answers and Scripture to heal my hurt.

Coming Home

The next morning, I reviewed what I had written the night before, and I wrote God a letter in response.

> *Dear God,*
>
> *I listened. I am trying to seek your answers. I am trying to transfer what I know of you to what I believe about you. I have let bitterness mask my faith in you. I have blamed you for my hardships and for my aching heart. I have accused you of not listening to me when I have been the one ignoring you. I have loved myself when I should have loved you. I have used*

worry as an excuse to hide from you and your will for my life. I have compared my life to others in an attempt to justify my sinful response to your will for our family. I have chosen anger over faith. I was wrong. I am not saying it will be easy, but God I want to believe in you again. I want to live for you again. I want to need you again and see you in every good and hard answer in my life. I want to recommit to you as your child and continue to train up our children in the way they should go. I want to love you. Thank you for loving me.

—Sam

I felt so different. My problems were the same, my home was still a mess, and my financial status hadn't changed, but I felt such a peace now. I was trusting (hesitantly) that God was going to do something awesome to save my family. I was scared, but I was putting my faith in God again, and it was awesome. I continued to read my (no longer dusty) Bible every day and memorize promises that God had written to me in his Word such as James 1:17, "Every good gift and every perfect gift is from above, and cometh down from the Father of lights, with whom is no variableness, neither shadow of turning." And one week, our family received a very good gift from above.

On a Thursday evening I got a phone call from Pastor Dave. He asked me how I was doing (what a loaded question), and I told him a simple "I'm doing well."

Then he continued to tell me that the church was having a youth service this coming Sunday and asked if I would please come since both of my sons were participating. I felt God prodding my heart. I got nervous at the thought of going to church again but knew I needed to go, and so I told him I would be there.

I told Jasper and Maggie that I was going to church that Sunday, and Jasper asked me if they could also come. I was thrilled at that because at least I knew them, and we could all cluster together. I picked them both up on Sunday morning, and the five of us drove to Sunday morning church together. We got there in the nick of time, so I didn't really talk to anyone before the service. Jason and Carter went up front and sat with the teen group. Pastor Dave introduced the teens, and then Jason joined a group of four other teen boys and they sang, "In Christ Alone." My heart craved the words I had never heard before,

> In Christ alone my hope is found
> He is my light, my strength, my song
> This cornerstone, this solid ground,
> Firm through the fiercest drought and
> storm.

What heights of love, what depths of
    peace,
When fears are stilled, when striv-
    ings cease!
My comforter, my all in all
Here in the love of Christ I stand.

After a few music specials from the teens,
Pastor Dave stood up and spoke again, "Now
I have asked some of the teens to share with
you some of the things that they have been
learning over their summer and just encourage you in how they are growing in Christ."

A girl with bright red curly hair spoke
first and shared how she had really been challenged to read her Bible more this summer
and had committed to spend more time in
prayer and the Word. I totally related to her
testimony and felt even more driven to continue in my reading and prayer life. Two more
teens shared testimonies of what they were
learning and how they were serving the Lord.
It was such a blessing to see these teenagers

publicly showing their love for God. Then my heart almost stopped when I saw Carter stand up to speak. I saw Jason shoot a look back to me to make sure I was still there and paying attention. What happened next, I will never forget.

Carter stood at the microphone and, somewhat timidly, spoke, "My name is Carter. I want to tell you about my summer. About two months ago, I went to teen camp with the youth group. I am not a camp guy and didn't come back one, but I did have one huge takeaway from camp. God loves me."

Carter continued to share the Scripture that he had shared with us at Jasper and Maggie's house on lasagna night. Then he continued, "I came home from camp feeling like God really did love me, but I wasn't sure how I felt about God yet. So Pastor Dave and Tyler said they wanted to do a Bible study with me. We studied the characteristics of God. I have learned a lot through talking with Pastor Dave, but what I wanted to share today is that two weeks ago, during our Bible study time, I accepted Jesus Christ. And I can now say that I am a child of God who loves me."

I fell apart. I actually gave out what sounded like a half-hiccup, half-gasp as I cried at the testimony of my son. In fact, it was so loud that half the church looked at me. But I didn't care. Maggie and Jasper both were tearful, and we all tried to keep it together through the rest of the service. I had no idea that Carter had been doing a Bible study or that he had even been reading the Bible at all. My heart was so full.

After the service, several people came up and introduced themselves to me and "my parents" that were with me. I would politely explain my relationship to Jasper and Maggie, but honestly, I think they would have been fine being known as my parents. A lot a familiar faces greeted me too. The one I was most nervous to greet was Stacey's. She had to have known that I was intentionally ignoring her and her offers for friendship and invitations to church. Stacey walked right up to me with the biggest smile and hugged me like I was her long-lost sister. When she stepped back, we were both crying. The last time I had seen her was the night Josh died, and I knew we both were remembering that in that moment. After a moment, Stacey just said, "What a wonderful day to see you again and hug you. I've missed you, and I'm so glad you're here."

That was all I needed her to say in that moment, and I felt completely at ease with her just like I used to. I introduced Stacey to Jasper and Maggie, and the three of them fell easily into conversation. Right at this time, Carter and Jason walked over to us. Part of me wanted to hug and kiss them and cry all over them, and part of me wanted to show exactly zero emotion so I didn't make them uncomfortable. I think I ended up with an awkward happy medium of side hugging them both and telling them I was so happy that I was their mom. We all three then chuckled at how odd that was that those two things just happened, but somehow, I could tell they both were beaming too. My family was healing. We were going to be okay. Pastor and Stacy talked with the five of us for quite a while after church; and at the end of our conversation when Pastor asked me if they'd see us next week, I was surprised at how quickly I said yes.

After church, we went over to Jasper and Maggie's house for lunch, and Jasper asked Carter a lot more about his testimony. He was so thrilled for him and was praising God for rescuing him. Carter was still reserved about the details but told Jasper much more about his Bible study with Pastor Dave and Tyler. Somehow, Jasper was able to talk to my sons in a way that I hadn't been able to. He was allowed to ask questions without getting the awkward chuckles afterward. I loved that.

And I loved hearing again about how
God was being real again for us.

Exceeding Abundantly Above All I Could Ask or Think

I n the next several months, a lot happened. I could see a huge change in our family and in Carter specifically. Jason, Carter, and I all started going to church together each week. It wasn't comfortable at first, and I didn't dive right in or pick right back up where I was when I left. I had to learn how to love God and be in church without Josh. That was (and still is) not easy for me. But seeing my sons flourish and grow with our church family stewarding them was amazing. In fact, Pastor Dave knew about Carter not being able to afford soccer camp, so he hired him to help build a deck in the back of their house and work on their old rusty truck their family had. Through these tasks, by the end of the summer, Carter was on his way to camp.

Jason continued working at the sub shop. He was slowly making his savings account grow for college, and I was so proud of him. Jasper reached out and offered to do a Bible study with Carter and Jason, and both eagerly accepted. Jasper's knowledge of God and his Word was so appealing to the boys, and the three of them together were amazing. Jasper was such an example and driving force for my sons to keep maturing spiritually and as men.

I felt so much growth in my heart as well. I began a prayer challenge with Stacy, and at the top of the prayer request list for me was still a new job. Stacy and I would pray together each week (sometimes on the phone if our schedules were full), and we would just cast our cares on God together. One day,

Stacy called me at home and told me that the church needed an office secretary since the current secretary was retiring. She asked me if I would be interested. I didn't know what to say. I knew nothing about being a secretary, but the job was full-time and would definitely replace at least a couple of my cleaning jobs that I had. After learning the details of the position and hearing the benefits, I accepted the job and rejoiced with Stacy over another answer to my "seeks" to God!

Maggie and Jasper continued to have me over once a week to clean and, usually more than that, to chat or have a meal together. They were family for us. And Maggie was not only my mentor, but my dear friend. I began praying for people as I cleaned their home and often would almost walk out the door without my check. It was so amazing that the one thing that kept me coming back to them in the beginning was the thing I now most easily forgot.

I continued writing to God. My letters were not always long and, often, they were still filled with cares that I needed to cast on him. The difference now was that I would take my (once completely dusty and ignored) Bible and seek its pages for the answers or promises regarding my cares.

I started my new job at the church once the boys went back to school in the fall. It was not an easy adjustment, but it was much better on my body, and I felt such a peace about it even in the midst of learning all new tasks. One day after a very long day of training, I went home feeling a bit discouraged. I walked up to my room and sat on my bed. I sat on my bed missing Josh and his encouragement I know he would have offered. That thought formerly would have been my prompt to be angry and shake my fist at God. But now I was trying to train myself to make that thought my cue to run to God's Word. I reached over to pick up my Bible and then stopped.

I turned and looked at Josh's nightstand. His Bible was still sitting there, covered in dust. I knew Josh would never pick up this Bible again, but I knew he'd hate it being a dust collector. I felt led to read out of his Bible. I thought, *Maybe it would help heal my aching heart for him if I touched the pages he once so eagerly sought through.* I reached across for his Bible and brushed the dust off. About twenty minutes later, I wrote the following letter to God.

> Dear Heavenly Father,
>
> Today I missed Josh again so much. I tried to focus on how much you have blessed us and how you have brought me back to yourself. I truly do feel such joy and peace now that I have not had in years at the least. But today was just tough. I picked up Josh's Bible today to read what you had written to me. I know

DEAR WHOEVER YOU ARE,

that you saved this for today. When I picked up his Bible off the night stand, a piece of paper fell out of the back cover. God, I cannot believe you have been saving this for today after all of these years.

The paper was not a letter to me, our sons, or to you God, but I feel like it is so much more important for me to have this.

Josh had written a list of prayer request for our family. I want to write them down here:

Carter—that he would grow up to be a man of God. That he would use his comedic personality and brilliant wit to draw people to himself and point them to you. That he would grow to honor his parents and seek you first.

Jason—that he would grow up into a faithful, confident leader for you, God. That he would continue to be an example to his brother and guide to those he will meet in the future. That he will learn to lean on you more than any other person including his parents. That he would be bold in his faith.

Sam—that she would continue to grow in her faith in you and that she would deepen her love for you and for others. That she would continue following you as she trains up our sons in the way they should go. That she would be strong in you and help me to remain strong in you also. That she would never doubt your will and that she would cling to your promises in difficulty and in peace. That she would always know you love her.

DEAR WHOEVER YOU ARE,

Me—that I would lead my family only direct their eyes to you. That I would learn to be open to change and closed to doubt. That I would have wisdom to make the tough decisions. That I would be accountable in my pursuit of you. That I would ask, knock, and seek you no matter what.

God, this is truly a miracle. I KNOW your Word is enough and that you will provide all my needs. But giving me this good and perfect gift from above has revealed to me once again that you exceed all I can ask or think. Thank you for this gift. Thank you for a loving husband, a loving father, but above all a man that loved you and prayed for his family to love you also.

Love,
Your child, Sam

Dear Heavenly Father

So much had happened in such a short time. Jason started attending a local community college and was able to pay for his first two semesters on his own. Carter continued to grow in his faith, and both boys became true servant leaders as time went on. I began growing so much too. Several ladies from church have become very intentional about mentoring me and encouraging me as I continue to ask, seek, and knock to God. I still struggle often with the "whys" of my life from the past, but God is showing me more and more the "nows" and the joy I am able to thrive in through Him today. I began seeing God in my life so much more than I used to and I know that a huge reason for that is that I am continuing to chip down my wall of bitterness and anger. God never left me, and when I fled from Him, he still pursued me even when I seemed unloveable. God is showing Himself strong in my family and in my walk with Him. I often claim the verse,

Psalm 40:2

He brought me up also out of an horrible pit, out of the miry clay, and set my feet upon a rock, and established my goings.

I know that God is actively bringing me up and setting me on solid ground as I walk with Him. I am able now to see how God is using my loss of Josh as very personal way to connect with others who have lost also. I have shared my testimony and struggles multiple times with those hurting in the church as well, and I have seen first-hand how God has used my own trial to encourage others and glorify him in the process.

A lot of joy and encouragement came along side some hard trials as well. Two years after I found the prayer requests in Josh's Bible, Maggie became very ill. Her frequent phone calls and cards in the mail stopped, but not her prayers. I still visited her often and would pray with her and Jasper for healing and for peace. She was weaker almost every time I saw her, so Jasper and I would usually just read the Scriptures to her or talk to her.

My sons came over to be with Jasper when about a month later, Maggie passed away in her sleep at home. I felt heavy with grief with the passing of this warrior of the faith, but I also felt such joy at the thought of her with her Savior in a place that was perfect.

Jason, Carter, and I sat with Jasper at Maggie's funeral. According to Jasper's wishes, Maggie was buried with two bundles of letters in her hands. One bundle was the letters

Jasper wrote to her before they were married. The other, much bigger stack was the bundle of letters that Maggie had written to God. I was so thankful that Maggie had, at different times, shared with me and even read to me what those letters contained. They were raw, genuine letters from the heart of a sinner to the God of salvation. They were her prayers.

Today Carter and I are going over to see Jasper and have homemade lasagna with him before we continue our study on Moses. Jasper has slowed down somewhat in speech and movement but not in mind. He still counsels us to this day, and I am always challenged by him. Carter has really become close to him over the years and often helps me care for him when needed. I have moved all of the pictures from the hallway of prayer downstairs to the living room for Jasper; and in a mint green picture frame with rhinestones in the corner, is now a photo of Maggie. Jasper holds her when he prays and says that he knows she would be praying right along with him if she were here.

We told Jasper goodnight and walked toward the front door. I told Carter to go ahead, and I'd be there in a minute. I walked down the hall to the office. The door creaked open, and the thick silence was somehow inviting. I walked in and sat down between the wispy white curtains on the window seat. I looked over at Maggie's desk and pictured her there. On her desk were all of her crazy stamps and colorful cards that she had been unable to use for quite a while. As I glanced around the room one more time, I noticed once again that bright yellow piece of paper on her book shelf that she had kept. It was the first letter I had written just to satisfy her that very first week. I picked it up and read it, shaking my head at the sarcastic tone I struck back then. I decided I had to write one more letter. It was addressed to God, but it was for Maggie that I wrote this one. I assumed my position once again and with pen in hand, I wrote on the back of the "old me" letter.

Dear Heavenly Father,

As I sit here and remember who I was the first time I sat here I am ashamed. But God, I am so grateful for Jasper and Maggie. You knew I needed them for so much more than a job. God because of the influence of these two saints I have seen my faith in you return. I've watched my sons grow to know their heavenly father and believe that they will see their earthly father again in heaven. Thank you for what I viewed as an old lady's challenge to write a letter to God. I am so thankful for the two people who guided me to only you. I still struggle with a lot. I still wish I had all the answers lined up, but when I have my days of fear, doubt, and sorrow I read my letter from God to me. And the letters that I once addressed to "whoever you are" became so significant in my return to GOD which is who you are. My Heavenly, loving Father. Thank you for showing me who you are.

Love,
Sam

About the Author

M olly Tomlins has always had a passion for writing and has poured herself into her first published book, *Dear Whoever You Are,*. With the firsthand experience of grief and loss of her dad when she was eleven years old, Molly shares personal insight through her writing. Her love of God and the people he has placed in her life is what drives her to write and share with others how God is growing her even in the midst of pain at times.